HELP

Why You Need Somebody (and Not Just Anybody)

to Guide You on the Long
and Winding Road of Investing

Arlene Alvarez

BALBOA.PRESS

A DIVISION OF HAY HOUSE

Balboa Press books may be ordered through booksellers or by contacting:

Balboa Press
A Division of Hay House
1663 Liberty Drive
Bloomington, IN 47403
www.balboapress.com
844-682-1282

Print information available on the last page.

ISBN: 978-1-9822-6911-1 (sc)
ISBN: 978-1-9822-6910-4 (hc)
ISBN: 978-1-9822-6913-5 (e)

Library of Congress Control Number: 2021910310

Balboa Press rev. date: 09/30/2021

*I don't care if Warren Buffet is
your financial advisor.
Power does not come from relying on
someone else to handle your money.
It is created when you—and only you—
take the initiative about your money.*

—Suze Orman

CONTENTS

HELP

This book has been in my head for years, and it has been a cathartic experience to finally transfer it to paper. I've had a career in the financial services industry for decades and felt so out of place with the shark-like nature of the environment. If the word "broker" intimidates you as a client, imagine how I felt as a working woman trying to navigate myself and my clients amongst this sea of predatory salesmen. Truthfully, there are good advisors amongst us, but there are also advisors out there who put their own interests before their clients'. It was so frustrating to lose a potential client to an advisor who either embellished or misrepresented an investment. It didn't seem right to witness advisors who were not being truly honest with their clients, without any concern that their actions may cause their clients to risk losing their hard-earned savings or miss meeting their financial goals. I was truthful, fair, and competitive in disclosing risks and fees. This transparency hurt me at times, since many advisors never even discussed these major details, mesmerizing clients with their intimidating, investment-lingo-speaking entourage and gazillion-page, labyrinthine presentations. It was also so uninspiring to be forced by management to attend unproductive after-hours meetings and dinners hosted by mutual fund companies that were eager to incentivize us to push their products. I was a single mom back in the day, when I got my start in the investment side of the financial services industry and will admit to having made every excuse in the book to be there for my girls instead of attending these unproductive "boys' club" meetings. I don't regret any of these decisions, and I am confident I made the best choices for myself by honoring my priorities and principles.

I have always had it in my heart to write a brief guide to help clients make better investing decisions and learn to navigate around the complex world of investing, sharing the knowledge I have acquired during my thirty-year career in the financial services industry. My goal with this book is to create awareness so that everyone can find and work with advisors and firms that truly care for them and proactively help them plan and make the sound financial decisions needed to reach their financial and life goals. I trust this book will be invaluable on your journey to creating the life of your dreams.

The best investment you can make is an investment in yourself. The more you learn, the more you'll earn.

—Warren Buffet

HERE COMES THE SUN

This book is dedicated to my Daniella, Gabriella, and Sebastian ... my sun, moon, and stars. You light up my life and I love you so very much,

Mom

I WANT TO HOLD YOUR HAND

*Real knowledge is to know the
extent of one's ignorance*

—Confucius

Everyone in life benefits from having their hand held to help them reach any goal. It amazes me how many people hire trainers and nutritionists to help them reach their health and wellness goals, yet the idea of working with a financial coach is a mere afterthought. Financial health is vital to creating the life you truly desire, and the magic begins once you decide to collaborate with the right financial advisor. Imagine the difference it would make in your life to work with someone who guides you toward your financial goals and holds your hand when you experience market volatility-related fear, like you may have experienced during the recent coronavirus crisis. The number one factor that affects portfolio returns is investor behavior. Most clients sell when they are scared and buy when they are euphoric about the markets. Over time, however, it's *time in the market* that creates wealth, *not timing the markets*. If you are presently enjoying the fruits of working with an advisor whom you love, congratulations! But if you are one of the many who are not, I invite you to invest a few minutes of your time and read this quick book, creatively set to Beatles' song titles. It may literally change your life.

How would you feel if you worked with a financial professional who holds your best interest at heart? Someone who guides, coaches, and inspires you to make the financial decisions you may not always have the knowledge or experience to make for yourself? I trust this book will *Help!* you on your journey to financial freedom and happiness.

BAND ON THE RUN

*When trillions of dollars are managed
by Wall Streeters charging high fees, it
will usually be the managers who reap
the outsized profits, not the clients.*

—Warren Buffett

My husband and I are both financial advisors. We met at work. It was the nineties and an exciting time in the investment business. We loved making money for our clients during the tech boom. Then it busted. We have been through 9/11 and the nail-biting financial crisis of 2008. Our heads are full of gray—a sign of having been tested by many crises. We have earned our stripes in the business and have seen firsthand what markets can do on the downside as well as the upside. We have also worked for large banks and investment firms that trained us when we were starting out decades ago, primarily offering high-cost mutual funds (which we now avoid like the plague) and other products designed to enhance the firms' balance sheets rather than their clients'. Everyone on the corporate totem pole has to be compensated (bankers, managers, etc.), and oftentimes clients get lost in the shuffle, paying more for less service, less experience, and limited access to an open architecture of investment vehicles.

Six years ago, I made the best career decision ever and took my practice to an independent channel, and my husband followed suit three years later. In retrospect, we wish we had made the decision sooner and are shocked at how much our prior firms took advantage of us as advisors and, more importantly, our clients. This venture into the entrepreneurial world has been priceless and eye-opening. This was just the beginning of all I came to learn as an independent advisor.

Investing legend Warren Buffet was mentored by Benjamin Graham, who authored one of the most highly regarded investing books of all time, *The Intelligent Investor*. I recently listened to it again on Audible and caught something that I had not really paid attention to the first time I read it. In the chapter on financial institutions, Graham mentions how big banks are not the best place for clients to manage their portfolios. He specifically goes on to explain how portfolio managers at large banks bundle client funds into their supposedly customized portfolios, delivering a lesser return in the long run. The culprits, says Graham, are lack of customization for the client and high fees. This book was published in 1949, and this observation still rings true today.

REVOLUTION

The secret to getting ahead is getting started.

—Mark Twain

There's a revolution going on in the investment world, and I am grateful to be part of this movement. The financial services industry is going through a massive metamorphosis, and regulations are finally being put in place to protect the best interests of our clients. Respected thought leaders such as Tony Robbins are speaking out and publishing books urging the general public to take an active interest in their money matters. Thank you, Tony! Too many people abdicate the responsibility of building their wealth, and the lack of communication, transparency, and integrity among investment advisors is costing clients more than money. It is affecting their returns, which in turn means that it will take them longer to reach their financial goals, affecting their quality of life and potentially their physical health. The number one cause of stress in the United States is money, and one of the leading causes of illness is stress. I meet clients every day who are uneasy about their portfolios. They don't understand what they own, why they own it, or how their advisor is compensated. In many cases, clients are paying too much for no advice (or worse—bad advice) and feel increasing frustration over a lack of communication, honesty, fairness, and transparency. Costs are only an issue in the absence of value, but in so many circumstances, clients are not benefiting from either, settling for less and as a result, receiving less.

There is a better way. Don't settle for an inexperienced or self-serving "salesperson" style advisor, who doesn't return your calls or educate you. There are honest and experienced advisors out there who can help you build your wealth, increase your investment acumen, and bring you confidence in the process. Like spouses in miserable marriages, many clients make the indecision to stay with their subpar advisors and firms even though they are not happy. You are not stuck with the financial advisor who is available to you at your local bank, or the one that you and your friends play golf with who is a good guy but has not grown your portfolio in a decade. You also don't have to invest your time and money in a course to try your hand at mastering the complex world of investing online (although there is a simple way you can do it that I will discuss later in this book). Don't wait until the next market crash to evaluate this important decision. Having a trusting relationship with the person who is guiding you toward financial independence and happiness is the key to building your wealth and helping create a fulfilling future for you and your loved ones. This is possible!

Like your relationship with your doctor, your relationship

with your financial advisor is one of the most important human relationships you can have. It all begins with identifying the right financial advisor for *you*. There are many advisors out there, and although there are so many titles to describe what it is we do, in the end what is paramount is that you find one who is transparent, experienced, educational, accessible, and trustworthy. Enjoying your meetings and interactions is also important, as you will be naturally be more engaged in relationships that you look forward to. Whether you have thousands or millions to invest, aligning yourself with a financial advisor who coaches, educates, and inspires you will make your life a richer experience in every way.

WITH A LITTLE HELP
FROM MY FRIENDS

*Wall Street is the only place that people
ride in a Rolls Royce to get advice
from those who take the subway.*

—Warren Buffett

The best way to find a reputable advisor is to get a referral from a friend or colleague. Just as you wouldn't ask an obese person for diet advice, your first choice should be someone who is in a financially good place with a similar risk tolerance. CPAs and attorneys are other good resources. People are generally very happy to recommend professionals whose work they are fond of. Be cognizant of the fact that many reputable advisors have account minimums. This is not necessarily a bad thing. These advisors are committed to providing a certain level of service, and they simply cannot deliver this excellence to everyone who walks in the door. Many have "invitation only" practices. In most cases, they will be happy to assist you if you are referred by an existing valued client and will be more than willing to point you in the right direction.

I urge you to be prudent about who you choose to assist you. Listen to your intuition. You will not do well working with someone you don't trust. Also, don't feel pressured or obligated or romanced into investing with a stranger. Keep this in mind the next time your bank teller suggests that you speak to their in-house financial advisor. Banks are great places to keep your checking account, but a seasoned financial advisor is not likely to be found at your local branch.

I know this from personal experience. In keeping with the spirit of full disclosure, this is how I got my start over twenty years ago. If a financial advisor can take you as a walk-in, this should be a red flag. Someone who is experienced and has a substantial client base is not sitting around waiting for potential clients to walk in. As an added frustration, you will forever be cross-sold all sorts of bank products every time you walk in or call. Do your homework, and work with someone who you are confident has the specialized experience to help you make thoughtful financial decisions to positively impact your life. Don't buy into a big-name bank or its plethora of products. Instead, seek to find and fully trust the person who will be coaching you to stick with your financial plan.

DEAR PRUDENCE

The years ahead will occasionally deliver major market declines—even panics—that will affect virtually all stocks. No one can tell you when these traumas will occur.

—Warren Buffett

It's scary to think about losing money, and I have seen many inexperienced advisors take unnecessary risks, trying to look like a star bankrolling their client's savings on a few stocks or volatile sectors. More experienced advisors would never do this. Your advisor should be working for you and helping you set up a diversified portfolio that is in line with your risk tolerance, preferably providing some form of income along the way in the form of dividends or interest. Prudent investing is not like playing roulette in Las Vegas. It is quite possible to lose a lot of money if you put all your chips on one investment (stock, bond, fund, or anything)—unless you got lucky and placed all your chips on a winner, of course. There is a well-known investment mantra that states "concentrate to create; diversify to protect." With a customized portfolio, you can actually do both. I typically recommend concentrating no more than 5 percent in any one position and no more than 20 percent in any one sector (I truthfully prefer to keep less and feel more comfortable around 15 percent). I value transparency and being able to see every position in the portfolio. Not everything is going to go up on a given year—or down—and even the most intelligent experts on the planet do not know what is going to happen. Investors cannot control what the market can do, but they can control what they own in their portfolios ... and knowing what you own and why you own it will bring you much-needed confidence when faced with an unexpected crisis situation in the markets.

GOT TO GET YOU INTO MY LIFE

*Better a diamond with a flaw
than a pebble without.*

—Confucius

If you were involved in a car accident and needed to be attended to immediately, would you prefer to be attended by a recent Harvard Med School graduate or a doctor who has been practicing medicine at a reputable hospital for over a decade? Experience is essential in this industry, and it is crucial that the person who is coaching you with your financial affairs has been through their share of market cycles. Nothing, absolutely nothing, can replace the experience earned through these financial traumas. In the ER of the financial world, you definitely want to work with someone who understands the risks and has the experience necessary to talk you back from the cliff when you want to jump and follow the herd.

Once you have identified a few potential financial advisor candidates (two or three will suffice), it is time to interview them. Any reputable advisor will also want to make sure that you are a good fit for them. Prior to your meeting, make sure to check the credentials of each candidate at www.finra.org. You can enter their name in the Broker Check section to verify their experience, education, and whether they have had any client issues. Although anyone can have had a crazy client or an unfair experience, numerous disclosures can be a red flag. Address any questions you may have regarding their experience, background, and the like during your meeting. This will pose a unique opportunity for you to see how they address this topic.

LISTEN

Predicting rain doesn't count,
building the ark does.

—Warren Buffett

During your discovery meeting, your prospective financial advisor should ask many questions about *you*: your goals, investment experience, appetite for risk, liquidity needs, income needs, and more. You should be doing most of the talking, and they should be doing some heavy-duty listening. She/he should also divulge the answers to the following questions, simply and transparently. If they do not, make sure to ask about:

1) What sets you apart from other advisors?
2) What is your investment process?
3) What investment vehicles do you typically use?
4) How often will we interact?
5) How accessible are you and your team?

6) What are your fees?
7) How often will we review my portfolio?

After your initial meeting, assess how you genuinely feel. Do you need this person in your life? Is this someone you feel you can trust to guide you along your path to financial independence and wealth? Did you enjoy your meeting? Do you feel inspired? Do you look forward to the next meeting? Like when dating, you hope you will be building a lifelong relationship with this person. In order for it to last, it has to be one where you are both growing, learning, and happy. Don't settle for working with someone who is subpar in this or any venture of your life. Working with a client/advisor you dislike is like marrying for money: it's toxic on both parts of the equation. Can you imagine how horrible things will get and feel when an inevitable negative market cycle approaches? That relationship will be even more strained and unsatisfactory for everyone.

I have met many advisors through the years who are always such Debbie Downers. They are always predicting a market Armageddon and creating much fear for themselves and their clients. In my opinion, if you are investing with that much fear, you shouldn't be investing, let alone leading someone as their advisor. Factually speaking, everyone knows that markets are up more years than they are down. Even those dreaded "down" periods can prove positive to the effect that they have the potential to present attractive entry points to invest or add to portfolios, adding to the momentum to build wealth. To lead clients, we can't be afraid. It's one thing to be prepared for a market crisis and another to be constantly missing the benefits of investing by encouraging fear. Bad markets do happen, but in reality, good markets outnumber them. If you work with an advisor who is thinking ahead and OF YOU, you will be prepared for the rainy seasons in the market. This will make all the difference in the world to both protecting your capital and your financial future during challenging times.

PENNY LANE

A penny saved is a penny earned.

—Benjamin Franklin

The number one factor that can affect an investor's return is their behavior. It's a natural human instinct to react to FOMO (fear of missing out) and to buy high and sell low when fear is rampant and the pundits on CNBC are preaching about a potential financial apocalypse. Tough times happen, but they don't last. Tough people do—and I expect you are resilient and committed to succeed if you are reading this book. There is, unfortunately, not much you can do about the world economy. Markets go up and go down. Over time, it's the ride that takes you to the summit. Sitting on cash doesn't. So, if you are an investor in your future, put on your seatbelt and be confident that the ride is taking you somewhere. It actually should bring you confidence to know that you can set it and forget it.

Conversely, the second factor that affects investor returns is one that you *can* control and one you should look at: *fees.* Too many investors are paying way too much. I believe that most mutual funds have high fees that are not justified for either growth (stock) investing and especially not for income (bond) investing. Although it is possible to invest in exchange-traded funds (ETFs) online, investors still have to use an advisor to set up an individual bond/fixed income portfolio. Bond and preferred-income ETFs exist, but most likely don't have the predictability that you get with an individualized fixed-income portfolio that sets the price and interest rate factors for investors at inception. Basically, you will know how much you will receive in income and when and on what date each fixed income instrument will mature or potentially be pre-refunded or called. Bond ETFs cannot guarantee that, and bond mutual funds are far worse, as they are subject to transactions the portfolio manager may make that may even make investors lose money—and all at high fees. A sound financial advisor is always with you on the quest to grow your portfolio. They want to grow with you, and their advice is always tied on helping you find the most cost-efficient way to manage your portfolio.

THE LONG AND WINDING ROAD

The key to a great life lies in shifting your focus from accumulation to contribution. The old saying, "he who gathers the most toys wins" needs to be replaced with, "he who serves the most prospers." Happiness is the by-product of a life spent adding value to other people's lives.

—Robin Sharma

There is an often-told fable about a power plant that one day abruptly stops working. The employees and owner are frantic trying to fix the problem, and the manager finally calls a local expert technician. After quickly checking the electrical boxes, he carefully studies the wires and screws and in less than ten minutes is able to restore the power plant to function again. Everyone is relieved and rejoicing. The manager then asks the technician what he owes him for his services. The technician politely replies, "Ten thousand dollars." The manager is shocked at his fee, especially since he was only at the plant for what seemed like a few minutes. The technician's fee seemed exorbitant, considering the fact that all he did was turn a few screws. The manager demanded an itemized bill. The technician then takes a pen and paper and itemizes his bill: "Turning screw: $1. Knowing which screw to turn: $9,999."

The point of this story is to illustrate the value of experience and applied knowledge. It takes decades to turn pro at anything, and this factor especially applies to the financial markets. Collaborating with an experienced professional who has been through their share of the long and winding roads of investing may very well be worth the value-added, fair expense, especially if they are generously willing to share their wisdom with you along the way.

PLEASE PLEASE ME

*Rule No. 1 is never lose money. Rule
No. 2 is never forget Rule No. 1.*

—Warren Buffett's Golden Rule of Investing

Every client is different, and so is each portfolio. It's crucial that both the investor and the advisor have an accurate vision of what they want their portfolio to do. Like your life, your portfolio should have a purpose to give it meaning. It should be customized to your needs, financial goals, and risk tolerance. Many of my clients invest for income, meaning that their investments have been selected to produce a passive income stream for them to live off predictably. Examples of typical income-producing instruments are bonds and preferred income securities. I may also incorporate some alternative strategies such as income-producing real estate investment trusts and income-structured notes. Some high-dividend-paying stocks may also be good options, but realistically investors need to be aware that companies can slash their stock dividends if they hit a rough spot, as GE did recently (in 2018). Bonds pay interest as scheduled and return principal

21

at maturity, as long as the company does not go bankrupt. This makes the case for investing in investment-grade quality bonds. Income-structured notes are alternative investments which can also provide high income annually and are projected to return principal at maturity as long as the underlying indexes or stocks are not down by the percentage stated by the note. With the right diversification strategy, an income-portfolio strategy generating twice the dollar amount in projected annual income than the dollar amount invested in any one position can handle the unlikely (but never impossible) event that one of their positions would go to zero in value due to an unprecedented or unfortunate event. This type of customized diversification takes more work than just dumping funds into a mutual fund or outsourced strategy, and I believe it is a more transparent, value-added proposition if you are an income investor.

HERE, THERE, AND EVERYWHERE

Money makes money.
And that money that money
makes, makes money.

—Benjamin Franklin

Financial information can be found everywhere you look. If you are watching CNBC, one minute you may watch a fixed-income-fund manager stressing how wonderful bonds are for preserving capital and producing income for investors, only to watch the next guest make the case for why equities are the only way to outpace inflation and truly grow your wealth over time. (Both statements are actually true, by the way.) Many financial magazines publish their annual lists of top mutual funds, while others rant about how expensive and tax-inefficient mutual funds are. Every investor's needs are different, and every portfolio should be as well. The return on stocks is twice as much as that on bonds, but not everyone is emotionally engineered to be an equity investor. Warren Buffett has so much money that he can happily live off the dividends from his stock portfolio, but you may not be able to survive with a 2-4 personal annual dividend return on the amount of money you currently have saved. There are so many ideas and concepts out there that clients can really lose their minds trying to figure out which strategy or platform is right for them. Robo-advisors and online trading platforms offer do-it-yourself services at low fees, but at what cost? I will argue that both first-time investors and busy professionals benefit from having an extra set of eyes guiding them towards their goals and helping them avoid crucial fear-induced mistakes. Many advisors today are offering one-time consulting services to help clients feel more confident about their portfolios and investment strategies. If given the opportunity to have a professional point you in the right direction faster, wouldn't you take it? Whether it be in the form of a higher income stream to you (for income seekers) or greater capital appreciation, the compounding effects over time are staggering. The quicker you make that positive shift, the quicker you will see the positive financial effects of that earnings momentum.

SOMETHING

A diamond is a chunk of coal that
did well under pressure.

—Henry Kissinger

In order to get something, you usually need to give up something. There's no such thing as a free lunch. Investors need to understand that they are giving up the stability of not seeing their portfolio values fluctuate in exchange for potentially higher returns and/or income streams. Income investors are giving up potential capital appreciation in return for receiving their growth in the form of income payments. Personally, I like to combine both growth and income to provide for a balanced portfolio diversification strategy, but there are some clients who seek 100 percent income generation from their portfolios in order to provide for lifestyle cash flow needs. These clients expect to receive their portfolio growth in the form of 4–8 percent annual income on average, depending on their risk tolerance and variety of fixed-income instruments considered within their portfolio. This income stream is distributed to their checking account on a monthly basis.

Basically, it's a passive-income paycheck. Although this cash flow can fluctuate, clients choosing this portfolio strategy can expect to receive a higher return on their money and are comfortable knowing that their portfolio will fluctuate on a daily basis to reflect the current market value of each underlying investment. This value approximately represents how much their portfolio can be sold for, should they intend on liquidating their investment(s) or a portion of it at its current market value. We teach our clients to keep an emergency reserve and cash on hand, so this should be a non-issue. All that is required is the mental muscle to understand that it is normal to expect that, based on their strategy, the components of their portfolio will fluctuate and that most income instruments within this portfolio strategy are designed to return principal at a set maturity date. Again, collaborating with a financial advisor will bring you added confidence, trust, knowledge, and understanding of these principles. There is no way to have an investment in the market that pays 4–8 percent consistently that does not fluctuate in value. Fixed annuities do not fluctuate in value, but they do not pay anywhere near that range. Bank CDs and money markets also do not fluctuate in value but pay less than 1 percent (currently). Clients considering these non-fluctuating strategies will have no choice but to eat into their principal on an annual basis as they slowly deplete their savings, since 1–2 percent is not going to provide the cash flow they need. There is no way to have your cake and eat it too, and it pays to get educated on your options. Your investments, like you and practically everything in life, have to do the work in order to shine.

WATCHING THE WHEELS

*How many millionaires do you know
who have become wealthy by investing
in savings accounts? I rest my case.*

—Robert G. Allen

Income investing is not meant to make investors wealthy; it's meant to help keep investors wealthy. Sometimes it can get frustrating for income investors to see that their portfolio strategy doesn't seem to grow. It does grow, but the returns are being paid out in the form of income and sent to their bank accounts. Consequently, these same clients are also quite happy during the occasional down markets, when they are still getting paid (continuing to receive their income to their bank accounts), versus growth investors who see their portfolios temporarily drop in value. There is always a give and take, and each investor's risk/reward ratio can change and evolve. Finding the right balance will come with time, experience, and their financial advisor's role in expanding the client's wisdom and, as a result, their comfort level and trust. Truthfully, in order to have some growth in the portfolio, investors need to consider some growth instruments that appreciate over time (stocks). They may also reinvest some of the income that is generated. Over time, stocks may provide for a greater average return as they have shown historically over time, especially for those clients who need to generate income from their portfolios and are comfortable with the volatility that comes with investing in stocks. Considering dividend-paying stocks may be a good option for those clients, since these stocks provide for potential capital appreciation as well as dividend income (2-4 percent). In the long-term, dividend payouts historically tend to grow, increasing the cash flow for investors taking the dividends in cash and compounding the dividend income for growth investors seeking wealth accumulation. An investment in your knowledge (most efficiently gained via collaborating with the right financial advisor) undeniably pays the best interest.

COME TOGETHER

*The advisory business is going to be there
forever because people need a mirror, a reverse
of themselves, to force them to diversify.
The relationship, even if it has tension,
between the advisor and the investor
is crucial. It always will be.
You'll never be able to robo this.*

—Kevin O'Leary

Most people schedule an annual check-up. It's beyond me why clients don't do the same with their investments. Like any disease or health issue that may make you feel uncomfortable, every issue is better managed when it is caught in time. You want to make sure you are working with someone who is actively watching over your portfolio as if it were their own. Ideally, you should have a detailed review once a year. Unless you are investing in a simple index strategy for growth (coming up next), you may be able to tweak your portfolio to help you create a higher income stream and improve the credit quality of your portfolio. Personally, I also collaborate with my clients' CPAs to help them plan for the upcoming year and make decisions that may help them improve the client's tax situation. Another tip is to surround yourself with competent, high-quality professionals (trust and estate attorneys, insurance specialists, etc.). It's the best way to help ensure you will achieve excellence in your results.

WE CAN WORK IT OUT

*Tell me and I forget, teach me and I may
remember, involve me and I learn.*

—Benjamin Franklin

Investors and advisors are both human beings. Fear and pleasure are the two factors that drive us to make decisions. Any time that you have concerns with your investment portfolio, it is imperative that you feel comfortable enough to discuss them with your advisor. Talking it out is an opportunity for both of you to understand each other. You both stand to gain a lot from these interactions, especially during a market crisis.

It's funny how investors don't obsess about their portfolio statements until we hit a major bump in the road. The recent Covid-19 crisis had investors studying every line of their statements, wanting to know why we invested in each line item and what each company does. Black-swan moments (unpredictable or unforeseen events) are excellent opportunities to learn and grow together. While many advisors were hiding under a rock, I hope yours took the time to call, comfort, and coach you during these times. These moments are stressful for both clients and their advisors. No client enjoys witnessing their portfolio nosedive by over 30 percent, and every advisor feels doubly horrible seeing that happen to their valued clients. Use these moments to speak up and connect. As an advisor, I appreciate it so much. It's like asking your spouse, "What is wrong?" and they respond with, "Nothing." The effort to communicate will pay off tenfold in the long run. Not only will you feel grateful that you voiced your concerns, your advisor will most likely better understand your pain thresholds and will help effectively position your portfolio accordingly. As a client and investor, you stand to gain the most by increasing your investing acumen. The end result over the years, apart from potentially growing your wealth, will be financial and behavioral wisdom, gratitude and peace of mind. Working it out together always brings you closer to your advisor and, ultimately, your goals.

ACROSS THE UNIVERSE

Know what you own and know why you own it.

—Peter Lynch

I don't mean to pick on the banks, but another reason I distrust them is that they are proprietarily wired to product push the most profitable investments for their bottom line, which are not necessarily the best for their clients. As I mentioned earlier, I worked thirteen years at Citigroup and ten at Wachovia/Wells Fargo. I learned a lot just by observing what managers were promoting to the field of investors. I quickly learned that the top revenue-generating instruments were usually first on deck. On the top of the investment menu we were served as advisors was mutual funds, insurance, and variable annuities. Following that were expensive trust platforms that offered the most horrible performance ever.

I am almost afraid to print this upcoming personal story. During my last few years at Wells Fargo, I didn't receive any bonuses because I didn't meet my quota of referring clients to these horrible trust platforms. We are not even going to mention the daily torment of actively avoiding all the bankers begging me to refer them bank accounts so they can keep their jobs. That scandal was very real, though unbelievable. I felt incredibly out of place in my career during that time, to the extent that I hired a coach to help me pivot towards a different profession and hold me accountable to start writing my books, so that I could get out of the business for good. This coach (thank you, Mimi!) helped me see the opportunity in my frustration and made me realize that what made me different was going to make me better.

At the time, I had not known any independent advisors. Literally a few months later, one of my colleagues resigned and went independent, and my path was suddenly made clear. My coach was working with Tony Robbins. For years I had been devouring all his books, including *Money, Master the Game*, where he mentioned principal-protected, structured products. In my ten years at Wells Fargo, I had never heard of them. These instruments are usually kept on the top shelf and are not mainstream at most firms ... and they are amazing! Although they are not meant to be considered for the entirety of a client's portfolio, diversifying with these investments is a phenomenal way to increase income streams and create a buffer to protect your principal. I learned about them immediately after I made the decision (one of the best of my life) to quit Wells Fargo and open my own independent office with Raymond James, who operates on a client-centric, transparent, low-fee platform. Simply stated, a stock, bond, fund, or ETF is the same everywhere. The key factors in having a positive experience come down to 1) a value-driven, enjoyable client/advisor relationship and 2) fees. Using an open architecture of more sophisticated investment instruments that are available within the universe of investing is a massive value add for clients, especially those looking for income or hedged principal protection. Going independent also exposed me to a plethora of other investment options for clients that I had never been exposed to at my past firms. Coupled with the freedom to help save my clients on fees, I could now deliver added value by offering the best of both worlds.

Having learned this, I want you to know that working with a firm that offers these more sophisticated vehicles for all investors like you (not just ultra-high net worth clients) makes all the difference in the world to both investors and their advisors. There should be a purpose to the positions in your portfolio other than to make money for the financial institution, and as a client, you should know what that is.

CAN'T BUY ME LOVE

*People don't care how much you know
until they know how much you care.*

—Theodore Roosevelt

I promise this will be my last rant on the big banks. Remember that as a client, *you* are paying for everything. It's no secret that online banks pay higher interest rates on their accounts than traditional banks. They can and will because they don't have the high brick-and-mortar costs of owning branches and hiring the people who work there (and never return your calls). The same applies to the men in black who work in those stunning executive corner offices on the umpteenth floor. More is not better, and as the client, you are paying for this. Don't be enamored by their temporary attempt to make you feel like a celebrity. It usually lasts for one hour, and you are stuck paying their high fees on whatever underperforming, confusing, fifty-page hypothetical illustration peppered with industry jargon they just presented to you. You are not dumb, yet they want to impress you with how much they think they know and how little you know, so that you sign on the dotted line. It's embarrassing, and you should not put up with this. It's not about what they know. It's about knowing that they care about you. Don't trade your hard-earned money for a time-share investing experience. Your collaboration with your advisor should help you grow your investment dollars and sense. A good advisor will enthusiastically teach you whatever you need to learn to feel comfortable entrusting them with your savings. They will talk to you in terms you will understand so that you learn, versus trying to show you how much they know by talking over your head and leaving you feeling stupid. It's a privilege to manage your portfolio, not a sales transaction, and it is a collaborative responsibility shared between the advisor and the client.

TICKET TO RIDE

*Don't look for the needle in the
haystack. Just buy the haystack!*

*The miracle of compounding returns
is overwhelmed by the tyranny
of compounding costs.*

—John Bogle

A bove are a few of my favorite quotes from Vanguard founder John Bogle regarding the value of simple, low-cost index investing. John Bogle created the first index fund available to the general public in 1976 and started the trend for ETF investing that is still growing today.

If you don't want to work with an advisor, or if you want to simplify your investing strategy for growth by just buying an S&P 500 ETF, doing it on your own may be your best ticket. You can open up an account at Vanguard, Charles Schwab, Raymond James, or any other independent firm that can simply handle your investments in a basic S&P 500 ETF. By definition, the S&P 500 Index tracks the stocks of 500 large-cap companies in the United States. While investors can't directly invest in the actual S&P 500, they can invest in ETFs (exchange traded funds) that simulate and track them. There is also a universe of sector-specific ETFs out there for clients who want to invest in a specific industry or sector such as technology or biotechnology/health care. These ETFs have substantially lower fees than their comparable mutual funds and are potentially more tax-efficient. The S&P 500 Index is the bar to beat for most mutual funds, and the majority of fund managers fail to beat the performance of the S&P 500.

The main difference between an ETF and a mutual fund is active versus passive management. By definition, an ETF is a basket of securities that is passively managed, hence the lower fees. By definition, a mutual fund is an open-ended, professionally managed investment fund that pools money from many investors (such as you) to purchase securities. Mutual funds are actively traded by the manager, and they carry higher fees to cover the cost of the fund manager (investment advisory fees), as well as shareholder transaction costs and marketing, administration, and distribution expenses. I agree with the likes of Warren Buffett, Tony Robbins and Suze Orman that for the most part ETFs are a better choice. If you google Wikipedia, you will find that the S&P 500 has averaged 9.8 percent since 1926 (current data as of this book's printing in 2021). This data can vary slightly over time (depending when you measure it, of course); however, it is safe to say that the S&P 500 Index has historically averaged over 8–9 percent per year, in a time span that includes the Great

Depression, the financial crisis of 2008, and the current Covid-19 pandemic. Warren Buffet, in fact, has requested that the Trustee in charge of his estate invest 90 percent of his money in an S&P 500 Index for his wife after he dies.

DAY TRIPPER

*Calling someone who trades actively in
the market an investor is like calling
someone who repeatedly engages in
one-night stands a romantic.*

—Warren Buffett

What about day trading? Everyone has heard the
adage that *time in the market* is what is important,
not *timing the market*. It's impossible to consistently sell
something at its highest price after buying it at its lowest
price. Day trading also really is psychologically daunting
and stressful. It's not for the faint of heart, and the damage
it can do to your financial stamina is worse than any
potential upside you may have. The internet and social
media are full of courses and seminars promising quick
and easy investment strategies, ranging from options to
day-trading penny stocks. It's all marketing! Although
it may seem like millions of investors are working a few
hours a day successfully trading and turning a consistent
high profit on their portfolios and becoming millionaires,
the majority are not.

Be wary of friends who claim to be savvy investors. The fact that they have the courage to day trade doesn't necessarily make them investment professionals. It's easy to get excited about making a quick and easy buck, but easy come is really easy go most of the time. I have no qualms about taking a certain dollar amount that you are willing to lose (key phrase here) and trading it, as long as you are fully aware of the risks involved. Ask yourself, *Would I rather buy Beyond Meat stock and see if I make some quick cash, or get front-row seats to a Fleetwood Mac concert?* If you look at your potential loss of funds that way, it may help you decide if taking this risk is right for you.

GIVE PEACE A CHANCE

*If you aren't thinking about owning
a stock for ten years, don't even think
about owning it for ten minutes.*

—Warren Buffett

A super-simple concept I teach clients who want to invest in stocks is to invest in companies that they simply can't live without. There is no such thing as a "stock tip." No one ever knows with 100 percent certainty that a stock is going to take off to the stratosphere, and by the time a one-hit-wonder stock doubles in price in less than a year, investors may have already missed the boat. This type of investing is so stressful, but like the shiny lights in Vegas, it attracts many due to the excitement and instant gratification, which can also lead to instant loss. I prefer investments in companies that I can confidently hold for the long term, no matter what happens. No one wants to lose sleep about losing a portion of their hard-earned savings, and this simple strategy may work for investors looking for long-term growth with little worry.

So many people talk about how they don't understand

how Facebook and Uber make money, but, truthfully, I think most of us would be up in arms if we no longer could use our Facebook/Instagram to see what our friends and family are up to, and we would definitely be amiss without the eat-drink-and-be-merry benefits of Uber/UberEats. The same can be said of Apple, Amazon, Google, Visa, UPS, Verizon, AT&T, and Microsoft—all companies that keep our lives moving efficiently on a daily basis. Investing is scary, and there are no guarantees ever, but sticking to companies that you would be confident owning for the long term will definitely help you stay the course. Should any of these suffer a price correction, the wise thing to do would be to buy more, since essentially the stock may have become undervalued—presenting an opportunity to buy more and potentially get a better price on these stocks. Keeping the mindset that you have committed to investing and growing your fortune for the long-term is also key. It doesn't matter if your investment is temporarily down. If you have invested in solid companies, they should all grow exponentially with time.

EIGHT DAYS A WEEK

*The investor's chief problem—
and his worst enemy—
is likely to be himself.
In the end, how your investments behave is
much less important than how you behave.*

—Benjamin Graham

Through the years, I have learned and taught that investing is really meant to be a commitment for the long term. Like physical fitness, commitment trumps luck every time. A little luck does linger in the crossroads of preparation and opportunity, but being consistent is really what creates results.

I have been a long-time member of Equinox Sports Club, whose tagline is, "Commit to something." I work out every day, and every time I see their slogan I think about how fantastic it would be if everyone would commit to consistently working on their health *and wealth*. No one is going to do your physical or financial pushups for you. But you can definitely create the life you want by sticking to your plan and investing in yourself. Goals are attainable when you break them down into consistent, disciplined

45

steps. Don't focus on the $2 million you want to have at retirement. Focus on the steps to get there, and stick to your plan and process. For example, if you are thirty-seven and are achieving an 8 percent average annual return (just under the average historical return of the S&P 500), you will be close to that number (approximately $1,971,828) by age sixty if you make the consistent commitment to save and invest $2,500 per month.

If you are writing or reading a book, you get to the end a few pages at a time. Seeing that book or project sitting on your nightstand is not going to inspire you. Taking daily steps to achieve your goal will. The same is true with learning a language, taking a course, sticking to a healthy diet, getting in shape, growing your business, or establishing any lifetime habit or goal. There is no magic pill. The formula is setting the goal and sticking to the steps and not quitting when times are tough. Anyone who has achieved their goals in life will tell you that the journey is as inspiring and exciting as achieving the final result. It's all about the momentum. It takes work, discipline, and consistency to reach any goal, especially those that can be positively measured in time, such as health and financial goals. Over time, you can progressively build your health and wealth with good habits.

WITH A LITTLE LUCK

Work hard at your job and you can make a living.
Work on yourself and you can make a fortune.

—Jim Rohn

L uck is nothing more magical than preparing so that the great deck of life is stacked in your favor. I always tell my clients that their top source of growth is usually their business/work and that investing can be a way to consistently compound their savings and create another source of income and growth. Other than winning the lottery, I believe there are truly only three ways to build your wealth.

1) Work. Working your way up as an employee will provide you with a salary/commissions and growth potential. Ideally, a more significant means to create career financial security for yourself can be achieved by owning your own business. Entrepreneurs can benefit from running their own company in a world that they know and understand, and great wealth can be created and passed on or sold. Not everyone is cut out to be an entrepreneur or has developed a talent they can market as an artist or athlete, and that's okay and important to acknowledge. Many businesses also require some capital to get off the ground: another potential barrier.

2) *Real estate.* Own a portfolio of real estate properties that appreciates in value over time and provides consistent rental income. Again, not everyone has the capital required to build a real estate portfolio, and investors in real estate also need to come up with cash annually to pay for property taxes, insurance, property management, and repairs.

3) *Invest.* <u>Anyone</u> can start building their wealth by paying themselves first and saving/investing. Employees of all ranks can invest in their company-sponsored 401ks or save in any of the methods described in this book. Business owners and artists can tax-efficiently invest part of their savings/earnings as well. I think this is such an empowering fact—to know that you can truly create your own wealth if you strive to follow the principles outlined in this book. You don't have be born with a trust fund or inherit a portfolio of properties or businesses. You can create your self-generated abundance by simply saving and investing consistently. Your worst enemy is not bad luck with the markets. The main culprit tends to be making emotionally charged, panicked or greed-driven decisions at the wrong time. Most investors feel compelled to sell when the going gets tough, taking unnecessary losses. If

you have enough saved in your liquid emergency fund (cash and cash equivalents, such as a money market or savings account that is not invested in the market), this will help you avoid the temptation to tap into your investments during a down period. If you are properly invested, you may even have portions of your portfolio that you can liquidate at a profit as well. Real estate investors don't have 100 percent success rate with all their rental properties. Songwriters don't always write number-one hits every time, and actors don't always pick blockbuster scripts. Every business owner or artist is not immune to the occasional dud. These need not be career-breakers or portfolio-breakers, just very minor setbacks. If you have the right financial advisor educating you to make the right decisions for yourself during the difficult times, this partnership can be a positive catalyst to help you stay the course and keep you in line with your financial goals.

LET IT BE

We don't have to be smarter than the rest. We just have to be more disciplined than the rest.

—Warren Buffett

As with almost everything in life, consistency is the key to success. If you are going to embark on the self-investing journey in index funds, the key is to decide on a dollar amount that you wish to invest on a monthly basis, then just set it and forget it. By averaging into the market on a monthly basis, you will also be averaging your cost as well as helping to eliminate the worry about buying at the high and missing out on investing when the markets are down. Whatever you do, do not commit the financially fatal decision to stop investing during a market correction. When market values drop is precisely the time when you have to flex your investment muscles and realize that you are buying your future wealth at a discounted price. If you can, I'd recommend setting up monthly automatic deductions to invest. Pay yourself first, and just let it be. All it takes is a little discipline.

A DAY IN THE LIFE

What you focus on expands, and when you focus on the goodness in your life, you create more of it

—Oprah Winfrey

Have you ever found yourself in a tight financial situation? Have you noticed that the more you focus on your bills and debts, the more seem to come in? During these times, it seems like we are prone to experience unexpected and definitely unwanted expenses—our dishwasher decides to break, you get a parking ticket, etc. This has happened to me personally and I will tell you that what you focus on really does expand. If you keep telling yourself that you don't have enough, you will never have enough. I am not saying that you should lie to yourself or live in denial, but you do need to realize that sometimes our fear takes over and makes our problems bigger than they really are. And the more we say to ourselves that we are struggling financially, the more the universe will keep showing us situations to validate that belief. After all, we want to be right.

The key here is to realize that success in anything in

life is a result of good habits. A call to create more money in our lives is simply a sign and a blessing that we are capable of creating more. So, how do we do this? First of all, you have to change the language in your head. Stop telling yourself that you are broke, etc. Replace those thoughts with, *I have everything I need. I have set up a plan to save and invest for my future.* and *I can come up with a plan to make X amount of dollars and a time frame to pay this off.* Instead of bingeing on viewing CNBC during a market correction and chatting away about your portfolio crashing, remind yourself that the downturn can potentially present an opportunity to invest and buy more of the stocks you already own and love at lower prices. Remind yourself that you don't need to sell your entire portfolio at this moment precisely and that you are wise enough to know you have to wait this out. Cut the drama and focus on the wisdom. Look for the opportunities in the situation, and collaborate with your advisor.

Challenges can prove to be the best times to expand your knowledge, portfolio, and discipline. Challenges push us to grow, and growth, as applied to any area of our lives, is the aspect of life that oftentimes brings us the most happiness, by empowering us and creating a feeling of accomplishment. Even though money doesn't guarantee our happiness, being financially independent gives us the ability to make our lives richer in many ways and help people we love to do the same. Growth of all kinds (financial, personal, spiritual) is a vital part of the human experience and the key factor to our joy and sense of fulfillment.

IMAGINE

*A journey of a thousand miles
begins with a single step.*

—Lao-Tzu

Perception is an interesting concept. If you think that the market is most likely a means to lose money, it most likely will be. I have known many people who have that mindset when it comes to investing. Most of them personally experienced a painful financial loss in their investment accounts that occurred during a difficult time in their lives. Divorce, death, loss of a job, theft from a business partner—any of these deeply disappointing experiences occurring during a financial crisis can leave a person reeling and permanently scarred. Some people panic when things are at their worst, decide they don't want to deal with it, are convinced things are getting worse, sell at the worst time, and hit rock bottom in every aspect of their lives. Sometimes I think humans just need to do that to spring back up and recover; but for some, this experience is so deeply embedded in their minds and hearts that they just don't have the courage to invest again. It's a psychological hurdle. In my experience, getting past this is possible. It takes time, patience, and a slow and steady education process.

Over time, an investment portfolio has been one of the time-tested ways that both investors seeking a passive income stream and investors seeking capital appreciation can successfully reach their financial goals. In fact, it has been the most basic way that much of America's working population has saved for retirement within their employee-sponsored 401K plans—proof that consistent saving and investing produces tangible positive results over time. Although (in my opinion) many 401k plans are expensive and limited in their offerings (this is changing, thankfully), millions of Americans have still been able to positively and almost effortlessly build their retirement accounts through all kinds of economic markets, by sticking to the plan to have a certain amount of their paychecks automatically saved and matched for retirement. If you can imagine it, you can most likely create it. Compounding investment momentum and time will take care of the rest.

LOVE ME DO

A leader takes people where they want to go.
A great leader takes people where they don't
necessarily want to go, but ought to be.

—Rosalynn Smith Carter

As we progress in life, we tend to increase our skill set, and with it the amount of money that we receive for the work we do. What differentiates those who have wealth versus those who don't is one important habit: *They paid themselves first.* I manage money for many retired teachers, nurses, policemen and women, and others who have created substantial savings for their retirement due to their discipline and commitment to saving a portion of their paycheck every month. I mention them because I want to drive home the point that you don't have to make a six-figure salary to do this. They did it, and you can do it too. They focused on setting a goal in place and saving a portion of their pay to invest in their future fortune. It can be as simple as that.

To be completely honest, I have often found myself behind the eight-ball. My parents did not enjoy their lives and died relatively young of cancer. Their lack of joy in their life impacted me. I want to *live* my life, and I haven't always had the means to do it. Since my mom passed away, I felt a burning desire to travel and enjoy life and give my daughters and son the kind of life that I wish I would have had while growing up. I have been guilty of living above my means at times so that I can take my family on vacations and experiences that have filled our lives with many fond memories. Although I consider myself to be a very disciplined person, I will also confess that I suffer from FOMO (fear of missing out). I wasn't totally irresponsible, but I will confess that I did not always plan for these vacations properly. Nonetheless, I consistently committed to religiously making my monthly savings goal. If you want to build your wealth, you've got to love and pay yourself first.

GOODNIGHT TONIGHT

If you don't find a way to make money while you sleep, you will work until you die.

—Warren Buffett

To start creating wealth for yourself, I would recommend saving and investing 10–15 percent of what you earn a year. Make it a habit. Everyone can strive to do this. If you make $5,000 per month, make an effort to put away at least $500. Do it automatically, so that you won't be tempted to spend it. Consider it your wealth accumulation plan.

In the past, I saved with my former 401K plan at the maximum dollar amount that I could. Some companies match your contribution, an added bonus. Now that I have my own practice, I save with my SEP IRA. No matter what, I pay myself first and invest it wisely and simply. Thanks to this discipline, and over time, I have been able to create the retirement account I have today. Difficult times have come and gone (especially during my divorce, the 2008 financial crisis, and our current global pandemic), but I have stuck to the plan. It's like setting a goal to run three miles on the treadmill.

You set your goal and start walking. If you want to arrive sooner, you run faster. The key is to always keep moving in a positive direction. There are years I am able to save more than others, but the key is to always save. I keep my eye on the prize. I want to have enough money saved and invested so that I can have a passive income check coming to me once I am sixty. It feels good to know that I can do that and it inspires me. I teach my clients to get inspired about the same thing.

Adjust the pace, NOT the goal. I want to inspire you to build your wealth and live a life that feels abundant with time, purpose, and meaning. I want you to create a life with much to look forward to and to feel reassured with the freedom that being financially independent offers—freedom to be generous to others, to say yes to travel, to take dance classes, start a business, contribute to meaningful causes, or to say, "Take this job and shove it!"—whatever it is that makes you happy and pushes you to grow and make a difference in this world. Once you set the wheels in motion, you will have less to worry about as you keep building and compounding positive momentum.

DRIVE MY CAR

The man who asks a question
is a fool for a minute.
The man who does not is a fool for life.

—Confucius

Just as you would hire a driver to take you places more efficiently and free you to do what you do best (running your business or spending quality time with family or important projects), your financial advisor should be helping drive your investments decisions to help you get to where you want to go most efficiently. If you ever get intoxicated or negatively equilibrated, your advisor will also be your saving grace in getting you to your destination safely. This analogy is an important one because, in all honesty, they can help keep you from making some mistakes that can harmfully change your life.

Goal-focused, long-term planning is difficult to master by an individual investor acting alone. Human nature struggles to differentiate between market volatility and genuine risk, often assuming that risk is mitigated when investment results are rising, when the reality is actually quite the opposite. Volatility passes with time, as anyone can attest who has ever liquidated their portfolio during a fearful phase, only to witness new market highs within a few months or years. Your relationship with your advisor should be a mutual beneficial collaboration. You should both learn and grow together. Delegate, don't abdicate, the important responsibility of managing your investment portfolio. An advisor should help guide you in the right direction. Don't let them completely drive your car. Clients should never completely relinquish the extremely important responsibility of managing their wealth to another person or team.

You should definitely trust the person who is managing your money, but you should also keep tabs on your portfolio and be involved in the investment process. Just as you would phone your doctor when you think something feels off, you should also check on your investments periodically. It's way better for us, as advisors, to treat a condition in your portfolio that may be causing you pain or stress when it is brought to our attention promptly. And, just as you would expect any of these professionals to prescribe the best course of action for you, you should also make sure you completely understand the risks and potential side effects of any proposed changes. This process is typically quite simple, and the happiest client/advisor relationships are those that embrace open communication and understanding. Ask questions until you understand.

LISTEN TO WHAT THE MAN SAID

In the financial markets,
hindsight is forever 20/20,
but foresight is legally blind.
And thus, for most investors, market timing
is a practical and emotional impossibility.

—Benjamin Graham

Investing can be stressful, especially when clients get mesmerized by the pundits on TV or what their friends are saying. The smartest people sometimes have gotten the path of the markets wrong, and no one has a crystal ball. No one on this planet has the ability to accurately and consistently forecast the future of the markets. I will repeat that statement, because it is imperative for everyone to understand. No one on this planet has the ability to accurately and consistently forecast the future of the markets. Be wary of advisors whose premise is based solely on performance. Experienced planners don't predict, they plan.

I once read a funny quote from an economist, who said, "Economic forecasting exists to make astrology look respectable." As history has taught us, random, black-swan events such as terrorist attacks and an unprecedented global pandemic can unexpectedly thrust our economy off its course. No wealth manager in the world saw any of these events coming, yet many advisors moonlighted as psychologists during these times, walking their clients back from the cliff and helping them avoid the crucial mistake of selling out of fear. Planning can be the key determinant to success, and we all have the ability to set a plan and stick to it. We can also use our logic to understand that the fact that our portfolios are down temporarily doesn't necessarily mean they are going to stay down indefinitely. Times like these are when a financial advisor can really coach you and help you navigate through good and bad markets and help you stick to your financial goals.

Watching your portfolio's performance on the daily can create unnecessary stress, but knowing that someone is keeping an eye on it regularly is comforting. This is part of the value of what we, as caring advisors, can bring to our clients. It doesn't necessarily take a lot of time, and addressing points of stress before they grow into bigger stresses, diversifying holdings, and rebalancing can reduce portfolio risk and keep clients in tune with what is going on. My clients love knowing that I am looking at it their portfolios often and giving them feedback and quick updates, especially when markets are scary. Frequent contact really bonds the client/advisor relationship. I often envision a portfolio goal with the client during these monthly reviews, where we set a specific dollar goal for the portfolio and work together towards it. I very much enjoy this practice, and it is exciting when we create and reach a milestone. Focusing on something, be it a financial goal or anything else, really helps direct intention and activity to move towards a positive direction. This is where financial coaching can potentially create a massive impact on clients' portfolios and their personal lives.

I FEEL FINE

Simple can be harder than complex.
You have to work hard to get your
thinking clean to make it simple.

—Steve Jobs

It really makes a huge difference when you are someone's valued client. I cringe when I sometimes hear clients professing how they prefer to sprinkle their assets amongst different firms. Why would you want to be someone's mediocre client? Your calls will not be returned as quickly, and your assets will most likely be better served somewhere where your relationship is highly valued and attended to. Additionally, when clients have their investment portfolio split amongst several firms, they run the risk that their portfolios may have unintended asset concentration, creating unmonitored risk. For example, what if both your firms had held Lehman Brothers bonds in 2008? Ouch.

To avoid this concentration risk, I always suggest that clients who insist on working with several firms verify that there is little portfolio overlap. This will definitely take a bit more time and work on your part. If you do insist on having two or more investment advisors, you may want to consider the option of sharing your year-end portfolios with your most trusted advisor, to make sure that there is no overlap. Year-end tax harvesting is another planning tool that can be more efficiently exercised with full knowledge of gains/losses in all client portfolios.

I understand that sometimes there is a specialized need that is better met with two firms (such as lending with a private bank), but at the same time it is important to evaluate how much that firm diversification is going to cost. The private bank may be lending you money at a discounted rate, but how much are they charging you on the portfolio they are managing? Always do the math, and make sure you are getting what you are paying for.

NOWHERE MAN

*An investment in knowledge
pays the best interest.*

—Benjamin Franklin

Some clients are simply enamored with saying that their investments are currently held at a big US bank or investment firm. At the end of the day, both the client and the advisor are paying for the designer bank/wirehouse brand. You may be sold (as we were) on the glory of having your banking, brokerage, and lending all at one institution, but do you truly feel that the firm you are with is the best at everything? My experience has been that it is not always the case. As Kevin O'Leary has publicly stated, his fixed income (bonds, etc.) is managed at a wire house, and he manages the majority of his equity portfolio via low-cost Exchange Traded Funds (ETFs) issued by his own ETF firm.

Every business has its niches, and the investing, lending, and banking business is no different. Wouldn't you want to have the option to work independently with all the available options in banking, lending, and investing without having to be married to one institution for everything?

One of the current trends in the financial services industry is the independent advisor movement. Many advisors are now opting to go independent and, like doctors and attorneys, starting their own practices. However, not every advisor can upgrade their practice via the independent route. In order for an advisor to make this change, they should have a sizeable and loyal client following—yet another sign of a seasoned and experienced financial professional. All this translates to a better experience for the client in term of experience, cost, and service.

I felt this independent route was the best decision for me when I made the change six years ago, and my husband followed a few years later. I really value the ability to choose and freely cater to my own clients, versus being forced to take on clients I perhaps would not have chosen at my other firms. I feel grateful for the clients on my calendar and love looking forward to seeing and serving them. I think clients feel this positive energy and feel especially valued and appreciated too. I couldn't be happier as an independent advisor, and my clients are happier too.

Another benefit of having an independent practice is the ability to uniquely customize client experiences and portfolios. One of strategies that I use with my clients is to open two brokerage accounts instead of one. I teach a philosophy of dividing the investment portfolio between an "income bucket" that houses more conservative investments such as bonds, structured notes, preferred income securities, and other income producing instruments, and a "growth bucket" that houses stocks and ETFs for capital appreciation. Most of the income bucket instruments are intended to be held to maturity and not traded—unless we need to make a change to our portfolio strategy, or an opportunity arises to make a profit for the client and increase cash flow. Additionally, investing in individual fixed-income instruments, rather than a bond fund, provides greater transparency and allows the client to be in control of their own portfolio.

We believe in both sides being compensated for our advice on products recommended. We want our clients to know that we are building their portfolios in the most cost-efficient manner for them and that we are on their side of the table. We also consider alternative investments for our clients, many of which are not correlated with the financial markets, and having both accounts set up can avail us with the opportunity to offer the most favorable option for our clients. Everything we do is in the best interest of our clients. Knowing how and when your advisor is compensated is your right as an investor and a consumer. Your advisor should deliver value for their services and at a fair cost.

MAYBE I'M AMAZED

Risk comes from not knowing what you are doing.

—Warren Buffett

Frequently I meet clients who are not happy with their advisor. Many of them don't understand anything about their portfolios—literally, not a thing. What's worse is that many of them don't even trust their advisor, yet they are afraid to make a change, opting to stay with an advisor they are not happy with, rather than taking the initiative in a more positive direction. The fear can be paralyzing. Some of them don't even look at their statements.

Investing can be scary, but the true risk lies in not knowing what you are doing. I often meet clients who are still working with their ex's advisor. They are either scared or too overwhelmed to look for a new advisor after the divorce, despite the fact that they often don't like or feel comfortable working with their ex's advisor. Others feel obligated to stay with their family advisor, golf friend, or advisor to the bank where they house their checking accounts and loans. I've also seen clients turn over their hard-earned savings portfolios over to their "brilliant" children upon graduation from college, and Spanish-speaking clients struggling to effectively communicate with a less-than-fluent Spanish speaking advisor at their local bank. This really happens!

I have seen too many cases in my career where clients did not follow their gut feelings and stayed with their advisor despite their unhappiness, only to later face the regret of getting caught in a bad market cycle or having their bad advisor replaced with a worse one. Don't take that risk. Make an effort to find and work with someone who helps you understand, learn, and grow.

HELLO GOODBYE

Should you find yourself in a chronically leaking boat, energy devoted to changing vessels is likely to be more productive than energy devoted to patching leaks.

—Warren Buffett

C hanging financial advisors is not as hard as it may seem. And it may be one of the most important decisions you ever make. Over the years, I have met many clients that are afraid to lose their private-banking status. They think they are benefiting from perks such as complimentary credit cards or bank accounts, when in reality they may be paying a premium for their investments and getting paid very low interest in their bank accounts. Your financial advisor's primary role is to help you make sound financial decisions. It is not to sell you banking or investment products.

Over time, building a relationship with an advisor you trust is a key factor in your financial planning success. Your instincts are often right. You know when you have found someone you can trust and also when you should run. In many cases, I have calculated the high fees some people are paying their bank advisors just because they are afraid they will lose their private banking services on their checking accounts or have to pay the annual fee on their bank credit card (currently being waived as a "private banking" perk). To put it in perspective, paying as little as .25% more on a $1,000,000 portfolio (typical Private Banking minimum balance) translates to an annual cost of $2,500 each year (and growing with your portfolio). An American Express Platinum Card costs significantly less. Having worked in the banking channel as an Investment advisor, I have witnessed so many unfortunate instances of initiatives that benefit the banks at the expense of our clients. You can make a change if you decide to. Clients at times create an obstacle course in their minds, thinking that the transfer process is difficult. It isn't.

DON'T LET ME DOWN

With integrity, you have nothing to fear,
since you have nothing to hide.
With integrity, you will do the right
thing, so you will have no guilt.

—Zig Ziglar

Some clients are embarrassed to hurt their former advisor's feelings. Don't be. As in a marriage, if you were very happy, you wouldn't consider leaving. More importantly, you have a lot at stake if you stay. You need to watch out for your interests and those of your family and work with someone who shares the same priorities. If you are not happy, chances are, your advisor has let you down. Don't feel guilty or bad about making a change. It can prove to be a vital one to make for your financial health, and it's actually quite easy.

YESTERDAY

*Surround yourself with people that
are going to lift you higher.*

—Oprah

O nce you have met with and identified your new advisor, she/he will most likely take care of this process for you. With a signed transfer form and a copy of your most recent statement, your old advisor and firm will become a thing of the past. They may contact you to ask why you are transferring the account, and you can choose whether or not to respond. The signed transfer form is your authorization. Evaluate your current situation and if you are not happy, take a positive step towards your future, and leave your yesterdays behind.

ALL THOSE YEARS AGO

The best time to plant a tree was twenty years ago. The next best time is now.

—Chinese proverb

There is no need to feel bad about firing your existing advisor. No matter how long you have been together, he/she had an opportunity to serve you and didn't take full advantage of it. Trust me, if you were a valued client, you would not feel that way! There is nothing wrong making the vital decision to someone who is a better fit.

I would typically recommend taking the high road and emailing them and letting them know that you will be working with a new advisor. You really don't need to tell them who it is and why, but sometimes clients will feel bad admitting that they have found someone that they prefer to work with. That is the simple truth and always the best answer. If you prefer to skip this courtesy, that's totally fine as well. As I mentioned earlier, the transfer authorization will get you on your way to your new financial advisor. If only divorces were this easy!

GET BACK

Lost time is never found again.

—Benjamin Franklin

The longer you wait to start a health/diet/fitness regimen, the longer it will take to get in shape. The same is true with your finances. Don't wait for the market to crash again to make that change. A person who catches cancer at an early stage has a greater chance of beating it. The same is true with your portfolio.

Take action now, and don't be a casualty. This is important. This is crucial to your future and that of your family. Despite the current Covid-19 crisis, we are currently blessed to be on the tail end of the second-longest bull market in modern history, which started in March 2009. This will not last forever, and it would be safe to say that we will probably find ourselves in a healthy and normal recessionary cycle within the next couple of years. If you are not happy with your current advisor/bank/firm, *now* is the time to make the change. The last thing you want is to get caught in a storm without having someone you trust helping you steer in the right direction.

BLACKBIRD

*It's not because things are difficult
that we do not dare,
It is because we do not dare
that things are difficult.*

—Seneca

As I finish writing-this book, global markets are recovering after a heart-clenching decline in reaction to the Covid-19 virus. You may have seen this coined as a black-swan event, referring to an unpredictable incident that no one could have foreseen, causing severe impact and consequences. This has been a very scary time for both clients and advisors, some of whom have been hiding under a rock rather than communicating proactively with their clients.

I know from experience that some investors (and advisors) are going to be negatively impacted by emotional decision-making and lack of guidance. I also know that with the proper diversification and emergency cash reserves, coupled with communication and financial advice, investors will continue to grow past this. These rare, black-swan moments are the pivotal moments when you most need an honest, communicative, knowledgeable, and experienced advisor—someone to talk you out of your fear to sell everything at its lowest point, taking losses that will take decades to recoup. A good advisor helps keep you from hurting yourself.

In the state of Florida, where I live, there is highway sign that states, "Safety doesn't happen by accident." This applies to your portfolio as well. If you are well diversified, and you know what you own and why you own it, you can weather the storm.

IF I FELL

If you cannot control your emotions,
you cannot control your money.

—Warren Buffett

You also need to be aware of the risk involved with every holding in your portfolio prior to investing in it, so that you can be prepared for painful moments like these. For example, if one of your investments went down in value by 5 percent, you would only need it to appreciate 5.25 percent to break even. That one is simple, but what happens to the numbers once the losses get larger? If that same investment dropped in value by 20 percent you would then need it to appreciate by 25 percent to break even. If it lost 40 percent in value it would need to appreciate by 67 percent, and if it lost 50 percent it would need to appreciate by 100 percent. Those last two scenarios seem quite impossible unless you are adding to the position, averaging your cost basis and speeding up the process. Seeing any investment in your portfolio drop in value steeply can be stressful. During the week of March 23, 2020, markets hit new lows. Investors were terrified, and the coronavirus pressed humanity's fear buttons. People all over the world had colossal concerns over their health and money (the two factors that cause us the most stress). Consequently, some top-quality stocks dropped in price and were seriously undervalued. Apple and Microsoft, for example, had hit fresh 52-week lows, and many wise investors picked up these quality names at attractive prices. Having a trusted financial advisor to collaborate with during these times will help you take advantage of these timely investment opportunities. If you wait for the fear to go away, the opportunities may go away also.

ALL YOU NEED IS LOVE

It is in your moments of decision that your destiny is shaped. With every decision we make, good or bad, we map out a certain path. When you make a decision, it not only affects your life, but may affect others as well—sometimes, for generations to come.

—Tony Robbins

Much can be said about a person's choices of where they spend their money and time. Everyone is different. For me, unique experiences with family and friends, learning, travel, fitness, dance classes, concerts, shows and books top my list. Some people drive a modest car and spend copious amounts of money on fine wine and dining. Others have a beautiful home but won't get on a plane. Everyone is different, and it's important that you have the financial freedom to do what you love. Material things are cool, but they won't bring you eternal happiness. Happy memories and a life of growth, learning, and sharing definitely can.

In my career, I have seen many individuals buy status objects that they can't afford, just to keep up with the

Joneses, only to be left feeling financially and spiritually depleted. Physical money doesn't make you happy. But I believe that it can buy you the freedom to live your life on your terms and, if you are lucky, inspire you to be generous with your time, talent, and treasure towards others—which is where the key to even more happiness lies. I believe that giving is really the secret to getting, and teaching is the secret to mastering what you have learned in your life.

I once read that if you love life, life will love you back. Don't pretend to like things or people that don't mean anything to you. Love everything and everyone in your life—even the challenges. Surround yourself with good people. Your life is too important to waste along toxic people or people who are not helping you reach your highest potential.

Creatives and all kinds of professionals hire coaches to help them get to where they want to go, and this is often the secret to helping them reach their goals faster. It's time you did this for yourself! The best part is, it can actually cost you nothing. The best financial advisors I know coach their clients as part of their everyday practice. Ultimately, if you love your advisor and the work they are doing for you, they will love you back, and your growing portfolio and financial acumen will be living proof. If you are motivated to create abundance for your future and have someone helping you watch out for your best interests, the positive momentum will also help keep you inspired. When you are working with someone you trust, you feel that your best interests are paramount—you feel like an appreciated and valued client, and this friendship and your experience can be life-changing.

GRATITUDE

This may sound strange, but I'd first like to thank the challenges I have faced in my lifetime, especially when I got divorced. I didn't want to be a single mom who couldn't provide for my kids and was scared stiff that my ex (who had wealthy parents) was going to buy the kids gifts and things I couldn't give them. In retrospect, I realize this was an unnecessary thought, but it did give me leverage to elevate and reach higher.

I went from making a small salary when I filed for divorce to six times my income the following year. I also had to grow exponentially as a financial advisor to attract more clients. This experience also made it possible for me to be an independent female role model for my daughters and provide for them to grow their many talents and travel experiences. As Oprah says, "Things happen for you, not to you," and I trust that many of you have also risen to similar occasions in your life.

I want to thank my husband, Jose, who has been my partner in every way. I love and admire you more every day.

I also want to especially thank Tony Robbins, whose work has inspired me on so many levels and helped me inspire everyone I connect with personally and professionally in return. His books, *Money: Master the Game—7 Simple Steps to Financial Freedom* and *Unshakeable—Your Financial Freedom Playbook Creating Peace of Mind in a World of Volatility* are some of the books I most recommend for those wanting to learn about investing. A few others are listed below, in case you want to learn more.

The Intelligent Investor, by Benjamin Graham

The Cold, Hard Truth on Men, Women & Money, by Kevin O'Leary

Women & Money:Be Strong, Be Smart, Be Secure, By Suze Orman

I Will Teach You To Be Rich, by Ramit Sethi

Invested:A 12-month plan to financial freedom / How Warren Buffett and Charlie Munger Taught Me to Master My Mind, My Emotions, and My Money, by Danielle Town and Phil Town

The Path:Accelerating Your Journey To Financial Freedom, by Peter Mallouk with Tony Robbins

FROM ME TO YOU

Lastly and most importantly, I want to thank my family. My mom always told me to pick my friends wisely, because they were the family we got to choose. I feel extremely fortunate to have been born into a family I would have wished for and having had three of my favorite humans as children. I also call family my loving group of friends and clients. I chose you all always and admire you for your hearts, minds, and souls. I am truly blessed to be surrounded at all times by people I love and cherish. As the Beatles would say, *in my life, I've loved you most*.

IN MY LIFE

Arlene Alvarez is an independent financial advisor catering to creatives, soulful entrepreneurs, women, and the LGBT community. She is passionate about inspiring others to live memorable and abundant lives, and she channels her efforts through her writing, speaking engagements, and her Enrichment Wealth Management practice with Raymond James Financial Services in Coral Gables, Florida. She lives with her husband and two dogs and is exceptionally proud to count her three adult children, Daniella, Gabriella, and Sebastian amongst her favorite humans on this planet. She also sits on the Leadership Board of Girls, Inc., a non-profit organization dedicated to mentoring and inspiring all girls to be strong, smart and bold and also serves as Co-Chair of 150+ Women Strong. Arlene is obsessed with music, dance, fitness, wine, reading, writing, learning, soduku, travel, and aiming to make a positive difference in the lives of everyone she meets.

FOLLOW THE SUN

I truly hope this book helps you consider taking that pivotal first step towards building an abundant future for yourself. I know you can do this! According to the late and great Jim Rohn, "We must all suffer from one of two pains: the pain of discipline or the pain of regret. The difference is discipline weighs ounces while regret weighs tons." Which will yours be? Take action today. If you need help, please feel free to email me at arlene.alvarez@raymondjames.com. I'd be happy to point you in the right direction.

Wishing you joy, love, health, peace, growth, and abundance in every aspect of your life always,

Arlene

Wealth is the ability to fully experience life.

—Henry David Thoreau

Any opinions are those of the author, Arlene Alvarez, and not necessarily those of Raymond James Financial Services. Investing involves risk, and you may incur a profit or loss, regardless of the strategy selected. Past performance does not guarantee future results. This is not a recommendation to purchase or sell the stocks or companies pictured or mentioned.

Alternative investments involve substantial risks that may be greater than those associated with traditional investments and may be offered only to clients who meet specific suitability requirements, including minimum net worth tests. These risks include but are not limited to: limited or no liquidity, tax considerations, incentive fee structures, speculative investment strategies, and different regulatory and reporting requirements. There is no guarantee that any investment will meet its investment objectives or that substantial losses will be avoided.

Investors should consider the investment objectives, risks, charges, and expenses of an exchange traded fund, an investment company, and variable annuities and their underlying funds carefully before investing. This and other important information about exchange traded funds, investment companies, and variable annuities are contained in the prospectus, which can be obtained from your financial advisor and should be read carefully before investing.

Raymond James Financial Services, Inc. /
Enrichment Wealth Management
2100 Ponce De Leon Boulevard, Suite #1178
Coral Gables, Florida 33134
(786) 631-3771

Securities offered through Raymond James Financial Services, Inc. Member FINRA/SIPC. Investment advisory services are offered through Raymond James Financial Services Advisors, Inc. / Enrichment Wealth Management, which is not a registered broker/dealer and is independent of Raymond James Financial Services, Inc.

Raymond James is not affiliated with and does not endorse the opinions or services of above-listed persons or organizations.

CPSIA information can be obtained
at www.ICGtesting.com
Printed in the USA
LVHW040813021121
702222LV00005B/110